A Treasure in Earthen Vessels

An instrument for an
ecumenical reflection
on hermeneutics

Faith and Order Paper No. 182

November 1998

Cover design: Edwin Hassink

© WCC/Faith and Order
150 Route de Ferney
1211 Geneva 2
Switzerland

ISBN 2-8254-1303-8

Printed in November 1998 by Orthdruk Orthodox Printing House, Bialystok, Poland

Preface

This text explores the complex, potentially conflictual but often creative field of hermeneutics, focused specifically on the hermeneutical task entailed in the ecumenical search for visible church unity. This exploration, carried out at the request of the Fifth World Conference on Faith and Order (Santiago de Compostela, 1993), is a part of the ongoing work of Faith and Order.

Hermeneutical questions emerged in ecumenical work already in its beginnings. The churches' responses to the Baptism, Eucharist and Ministry text made it especially clear that Faith and Order needed to reflect on what is involved when authors, readers and interpreters of ecumenical documents come from many different contexts and confessions. The significance of the hermeneutical task for the ecumenical movement has deepened and widened since this initial perception. Indeed, representatives of churches from all parts of the world who participated in the Santiago conference made it clear that the work of Faith and Order could progress fruitfully only with serious exploration of the hermeneutical issues.

This text is the product of three study consultations (Dublin 1994, Lyons 1996 and Bossey 1997), and two small drafting meetings (Boston 1994 and Faverges 1998). Participants in these gatherings included members of the World Council of Churches' Commission on Faith and Order, joined by scholars particularly interested in hermeneutical questions. Participants came from all parts of the world and represented many ecclesial traditions (e.g. Anglican, Anabaptist/Pietist, Lutheran, Methodist, Old Catholic, Orthodox, Reformed, Roman Catholic). Interim versions were reviewed and critiqued at various stages by the Board of Faith and Order and by its Plenary Commission meeting in Moshi, Tanzania, in 1996. They have also been studied and responded to by a number of scholars in the field. Each and every response along the way has received careful attention.

It is hoped that the present text will be helpful to:

- *groups and committees preparing and responding to ecumenical documents;*
- *councils of churches creating study programmes;*
- *ecumenical officers and ecumenical committees of churches developing interchurch relations;*
- *persons who exercise a ministry of oversight;*
- *local churches and their ministers;*
- *teachers of ecumenism.*

In each instance, persons and groups are invited to take into consideration the exploration of ecumenical hermeneutics begun here. One of the best ways to receive this text is to use it to develop hermeneutical guidelines and other study materials appropriate to particular confessional, ecumenical and contextual settings. The ultimate hope is to assist in witnessing to the "treasure" which we have from God "in earthen vessels".

TABLE OF CONTENTS

Introduction

INTRODUCTION

1.   The unsearchable mystery of God's love was made manifest, through the power of the Holy Spirit, in the covenant with Israel and fully revealed in the life, death and resurrection of Jesus Christ. This mystery has been proclaimed in the Scriptures of the Old and New Testaments. Christian faith is the saving gift from God, which enables believers to receive the good news of God's love for all human beings and to become children of God and members of Christ's body the Church. Faith in Christ gives life to the communion (*koinonia*) of the Church. This faith has been handed on and received since apostolic times, from one generation to the next and from culture to culture.

2.   This transmission takes place within the ambiguities of human history and the challenges of daily Christian life. So Paul can speak of us as having "this treasure in earthen vessels" (2 Cor 4:7). Thus faith also relies upon human forms of expression and interpretation, dialogue and communication, all of which are fragile and all too often fragmented embodiments, none of which is completely adequate, of the mystery which has been revealed. These manifold human forms of expression include not only texts but also symbols and rites, stories and practices. Only at the end of time will the Church's contemplation of God's revealed mystery go beyond a partial knowledge and arrive at that "knowing even as we are known" of which Paul writes in 1 Cor 13:9-12.

3.   Unity in confessing the faith is among the essential ways in which the *koinonia* of the Church is made visible. The ecumenical movement has helped divided Christian communities to realize that even now they are united in a "growing, real though still imperfect *koinonia*" (Santiago de Compostela, 1993). This realization, however, cannot obscure the fact that significant differences in interpreting the faith still remain. In order to fulfil their vocation to grow in communion, the churches need to reflect together about the various ways in which the faith is expressed and interpreted.

4.   The unprecedented changes occurring in our times because of the developments in mass media and in the means of communication make Christians more acutely aware of the religious, cultural, political and economic diversities which characterize the human family.   The community of believers must formulate its faith anew within such contexts.   In this sense the mission to proclaim the Gospel in terms meaningful to people of today is essentially an hermeneutical task. All churches share the challenge of proclaiming God's Word in credible ways within the diversity of contemporary cultures and by means of the oral and visual instruments of communication, be they traditional or those made available by contemporary technology.

1.   The task of ecumenical hermeneutics

5.   The particular purpose of this text is to explore the potential of *ecumenical* hermeneutics.   Ecumenical hermeneutics shares with other forms of hermeneutics the goal of facilitating interpretation, communication and reception of texts, symbols and practices which give shape and meaning to particular communities.   In recent years the definitions of hermeneutics have multiplied in philosophy and theology, and the scope of the term has been widened beyond giving principles for the interpretation of Holy Scripture.   In this text we take the term hermeneutics to mean both *the art of interpretation and application of texts, symbols and practices in the present and from the past,* and *the theory about the methods of such interpretation and application.*[1]

---

[1]   The following definitions, drawn from recently published scholarly dictionaries of philosophy, illustrate a certain degree of consensus within the scientific literature on the topic. E.g., Hermeneutics: "The method of interpretation, first of texts, and secondly of the whole social, historical and psychological world" (*Oxford Dictionary of Philosophy*, Oxford 1994); "The art or theory of interpretation, or ...the interaction between interpreter and text that is part of the history of what is understood" (*Cambridge Dictionary of Philosophy*, Cambridge 1995); "A methodology of the right understanding and the meaningful explication and application of texts" (*Europäische Enzyklopädie zu Philosophie und Wissenschaften*, Hamburg 1990).

More specifically, *theological* hermeneutics concerns itself with texts, symbols, and practices which have been inherited and shaped within a tradition of faith. For Christians this tradition of faith includes the Scriptures of the Old and the New Testaments and the expressions of the Christian faith transmitted and re-expressed through the centuries. Within theological hermeneutics, *ecumenical* hermeneutics serves the specific task of focusing on how texts, symbols and practices in the various churches may be interpreted, communicated and mutually received as the churches engage in dialogue. In this sense it is a hermeneutics for the unity of the Church.

6.   The process of hermeneutical reflection impels and enables a living and faithful re-reading of any given text, symbol, or practice. A hermeneutics for unity should

•   aim at greater coherence in the interpretation of the faith and in the community of all believers as their voices unite in common praise of God;

•   make possible a mutually recognizable (re)appropriation of the sources of the Christian faith; and

•   prepare ways of common confession and prayer in spirit and truth.

Such an interpretation, which seeks to manifest the integral unity of the Christian faith and community, has been called *"hermeneutics of coherence"*. At the same time the process of hermeneutical reflection reveals the time-bound character of the traditional forms and formulations as well as any ambiguous or vested interests on the part of the interpreters both past and present. This means that the interpreters should also be interpreted. This critical and testing aspect of the hermeneutical task is known as "hermeneutics of suspicion". In a constantly ongoing process, a responsible ecumenical hermeneutics will try to serve the truth, alerted by suspicion but always aiming at coherence.

7.   The Church is called to be an *hermeneutical community*, that is, a community within which there is a commitment to explore and interpret anew the given texts, symbols and practices. The tasks of an hermeneutical community also include overcoming misunderstandings,

controversies and divisions; identifying dangers; resolving conflicts; and preventing schisms predicated on divisive interpretations of the Christian faith. The needs of the people of God in ever-new circumstances of faithful life and witness are also integral to this task. As an hermeneutical community, the Church also submits itself to being interpreted by the ever-challenging Word of God.

8.   This applies to each and every local church, and is a constant challenge within each confessional family of churches. As the churches engage in dialogue in the growing communion of churches in the ecumenical movement, a further and wider hermeneutical community is created. As it engages in ecumenical dialogue each church and tradition opens itself to being interpreted by other churches and traditions. To listen to the other does not necessarily mean to accept what other churches say, but to reckon with the possibility that the Spirit speaks within and through the others. This might be called *"hermeneutics of confidence"*. A hermeneutics for unity should entail an ecumenical method whereby Christians from various cultures and contexts, as well as different confessions, may encounter one another respectfully, always open to a *metanoia* which is a true "change of mind" and heart.

9.   The ecumenical movement provides particular opportunities for the churches to reflect together on issues of interpretation and communication for the sake of ecclesial unity and the renewal of human community.   But immediately it becomes clear that many Christian divisions are themselves based on conflicting interpretations of the texts, symbols and practices of the Christian faith. If we reflect together and agree on how traditions are to be interpreted, then the divisions of the churches - both those of longstanding character and new ones - might be better understood and even overcome. In this way, common reflection about our interpretations serves the "charism of truth" which has been entrusted to the people of God and its apostolic ministry. As a common ecclesial exercise of the gift of discernment, this reflection reveals the salvific power of the Holy Spirit in making known the Gospel and in uniting us with God. It brings into clearer focus the Spirit's own message, by resolving conflicts and preventing schisms, by sharing insights among

churches, and by responding to the needs and questions of the people of God in our contemporary circumstances.

10.   The need for hermeneutical reflection is not peculiar to our own age. Throughout the history of Christianity, diverse forms of interpretation have been used by different churches and denominations within various cultures and contexts. Given the wealth of cultural and linguistic differences, given the various structures of decision-making and the many ways of reading the Scriptures which have appeared over time and, perhaps most importantly, given the unsearchable mystery of God which surpasses any human expression, one can only rejoice in much of the diversity in the interpretation and practice of the apostolic faith. We need to acknowledge that the hidden mystery of God is revealed to us in manifold ways and we need together to recognise the variety of ways in which that mystery has been and is understood, expressed and lived. At the same time, for the sake of coherence of the faith and the unity of the community, a common understanding of the interpretative process is crucial for enabling the churches to affirm together their common Christian identity and to be open to what the Spirit is saying through the faith, life and witness of one another.[2]

2.   The origins of this study

11.   Reflection about hermeneutics arises with fresh urgency at this moment in the history of the ecumenical movement. A new climate of trust and mutual accountability has been nurtured, but at the same time there are hesitations and even retreats because churches are not clear about the meaning of ongoing work toward visible unity. The past thirty years of Faith and Order dialogue, as well as the dialogues of other multi- and bi-lateral commissions, have produced numerous convergence texts and agreements directed toward a common understanding of the Gospel and the Church, including its creeds, sacraments, and ministry. Yet many questions remain.   In our present situation, the impossibility of eucharistic sharing is felt with pain by many Christians. In particular, the

---

[2]   cf. BEM, Ministry 52.

texts *Baptism, Eucharist and Ministry*; *Confessing the One Faith* and *Church and World* have raised hermeneutical questions for the life of the churches. The process of officially responding to BEM has revealed many unexamined hermeneutical assumptions underlying not only the churches' responses but also the very question concerning the extent to which they can recognize in the BEM-text the faith of the Church through the ages.[3] The fresh urgency to reflect together about hermeneutics is further heightened as new challenges of Christian living in today's world threaten to create new schisms within as well as among churches.

12. While describing the present situation among divided Christian communities as one of a "growing, real though still imperfect *koinonia*," the Fifth World Conference of Faith and Order in Santiago de Compostela (1993) pointed to three different, yet related tasks which are vital to furthering such growth:

• to overcome and to reconcile the criteriological differences with regard to a faithful interpretation of the one Gospel, recognizing the multiform richness and diversity of the Canon of the Scriptures, as it is read, explicated and applied in the life of the churches, but at the same time strengthening the awareness of the one Tradition within the many traditions;[4]

• to express and communicate the one Gospel in and across various, sometimes even conflicting contexts, cultures and locations;[5]

• to work toward mutual accountability, discernment and authoritative teaching and towards credibility in common witness

---

[3] cf. *Baptism, Eucharist and Ministry 1982-1990: Report on the Process and the Responses,* Faith and Order Paper No. 149, WCC Geneva 1990, pp. 32-35.

[4] cf. *On the Way to Fuller Koinonia: Official Report of the Fifth World Conference on Faith and Order,* Thomas F. Best and Günther Gassmann (eds.), Faith and Order Paper No. 166, WCC Geneva 1994, Section II, para. 18, p. 241.

[5] *Ibid.,* Section I, para's 15-16, p. 232.

before the world, and finally towards the eschatological fullness of the truth in the power of the Holy Spirit.[6]

13. The present text will address these three tasks in the following way:

- In the first section (**A. Common Understanding of the One Tradition**) an explicitly hermeneutical framework will be applied to the important themes raised by the Montreal study "Scripture, Tradition and traditions". This reflection may take us beyond Montreal, as it considers the interpretation of Scripture and tradition in a more hermeneutically conscious way, especially with greater sensitivity to the conditions involved in interpretation.

- In the second section (**B. One Gospel in Many Contexts**) the text explores the hermeneutical and theological significance of the fact that the ecumenical movement includes the participation of communities from many differing cultures and contexts, and offers reflections which can lead to a more successful inter-contextual dialogue.

- The third section (**C. The Church as an hermeneutical Community**) explores three dimensions of the process of interpretation: the activity of discernment, the exercise of authority and the task of reception.

---

[6] *Ibid.*, Section III, para 31, pp. 251f., and Section IV, para. 3, p. 254.

A. COMMON UNDERSTANDING OF THE ONE TRADITION

1. Past exploration of the theme

14. From the World Council of Churches, from the Christian World Communions and from bi-lateral dialogues, as well as from the councils of each church, a great deal of agreed theological reflection has been produced in the past century. There is always a danger of ecumenical "loss of memory". Those engaged in the interpreting process need to use the original documents as well as the many explanatory books and pamphlets that make available ecumenical agreements. Particularly relevant from past exploration for the present task is the Fourth World Conference on Faith and Order.

15. The Fourth World Conference on Faith and Order at Montreal (1963), was able to say:

> By *the Tradition* is meant the Gospel itself, transmitted from generation to generation in and by the Church, Christ Himself present in the life of the Church. By *tradition* is meant the traditionary process. The term *traditions* is used...to indicate both the diversity of forms of expression and also what we call confessional traditions, for instance the Lutheran tradition or the Reformed tradition...the word appears in a further sense, when we speak of cultural traditions. (Section II, para. 39.)

> Our starting point is that we as Christians are all living in a tradition which goes back to our Lord and has its roots in the Old Testament and are all indebted to that tradition inasmuch as we have received the revealed truth, the Gospel, through its being transmitted from one generation to another. Thus we can say that we exist as Christians by the Tradition of the Gospel (the *paradosis* of the *kerygma*) testified in Scripture, transmitted in and by the Church, through the power of the Holy Spirit. (Section II, para. 45.)

> The traditions in Christian history are distinct from, and yet connected with, the Tradition. They are the expressions and manifestations in diverse historical terms of the one truth and reality which is Christ. This evaluation of the traditions poses serious problems...How can we distinguish between traditions embodying the true Tradition and merely human traditions? (Section II, para's 47 and 48.)

16.   Montreal thereby helped the churches to begin to realize that the one Tradition is witnessed to in Scripture and transmitted by the Holy Spirit through the Church. This means the canon of Scripture came into being within the Tradition, which finds expression within the various traditions of the Church. In this way Montreal helped to overcome the old contrast between "sola Scriptura" and "Scripture and tradition" and to show that the different hermeneutical criteria in the different traditions belong together. The ongoing interaction between Tradition and traditions enables faithful transmission, even though from time to time there have been distortions of the apostolic faith.

17.   But Montreal did not fully explain what it means that the one Tradition is embodied in concrete traditions and cultures. Concerning the quest for an hermeneutical principle the conference listed the different ways in which the various churches deal with this problem but did not itself deal with criteriological questions, such as how to discern the authenticity of faith in a situation of conflicting cultural perspectives, frameworks or hermeneutical principles.[8] Finally, Montreal could go no further than the WCC's Toronto Statement (1950), which deliberately

---

[8] Cf. Scripture, Tradition and Traditions, para. 53, in: P.C. Rodger and L. Vischer (ed.), *The Fourth World Conference on Faith and Order, Montreal 1963,* Faith and Order Paper No.42, SCM Press LTD, London 1964, p.53:
"In some confessional traditions the accepted hermeneutical principle has been that any portion of Scripture is to be interpreted in the light of Scripture as a whole. In others the key has been sought in what is considered to be the centre of Holy Scripture, and the emphasis has been primarily on the Incarnation, or on the Atonement and Redemption, or on justification by faith, or again on the message of the nearness of the Kingdom of God, or on the ethical teachings of Jesus. In yet others, all emphasis is laid upon what Scripture says to the individual conscience, under the guidance of the Holy Spirit. In the Orthodox Church the hermeneutical key is found in the mind of the Church, especially as expressed in the Fathers of the Church and in the Ecumenical Councils. In the Roman Catholic Church the key is found in the deposit of faith, of which the Church's magisterium is the guardian. In other traditions again the creeds, complemented by confessional documents or by the definitions of Ecumenical Councils and the witness of the Fathers, are considered to give the right key to the understanding of Scripture. In none of these cases where the principle of interpretation is found elsewhere than in Scripture is the authority thought to be alien to the central concept of Holy Scripture. On the contrary, it is considered as providing just a key to the understanding of what is said in Scripture."

provided no criteria beyond the "Basis" of the WCC[8] to assess the authenticity or fidelity of the traditions of its member churches, to say nothing of other human traditions. It could only point to the three main factors in the transmission process: the events and testimonies preceding and leading to Scripture, Scripture itself, and subsequent ecclesial preaching and teaching.

18. It must be recognized that Montreal left open the vital question of how churches can discern the one Tradition. Therefore there is a danger that churches identify the one Tradition exclusively with their own tradition. Even the discussion of this question in languages other than English is difficult, because the Montreal "solution" relied on English language conventions about the use of capital letters and these conventions can produce ambiguity, e.g. at the beginning of a sentence where it is not clear whether the capital letter distinguishes the one Tradition or simply marks the start of the sentence. These acknowledged limitations do not alter the fact that Montreal provided a valid set of distinctions, between Tradition as that which God intends to have handed on in the life of the Church, tradition as the process by which this handing on takes place and traditions as particular expressions of Christian life and thought. These exist in some tension with one another but can also be the vehicles for developing a deeper grasp of the one Tradition, by which is meant the one Gospel, the living Word of God.

19. After Montreal, Faith and Order undertook important studies on the hermeneutical significance of the Councils of the Early Church.[9] Several reports on the Authority of the Bible were assembled as a

---

[8] The Basis of the WCC's constitution reads: "The World Council of Churches is a fellowship of churches which confess the Lord Jesus Christ as God and Saviour according to the scriptures and therefore seek to fulfil together their common calling to the glory of the one God, Father, Son and Holy Spirit."

[9] "The Importance of the Conciliar Process in the Ancient Church for the Ecumenical Movement", in: *New Directions in Faith and Order, Bristol 1967*, Faith and Order Paper No. 50, Geneva 1968, pp. 49-59 (also in: *Councils and the Ecumenical Movement*, World Council Studies No. 5, WCC Geneva 1968).

contribution to the hermeneutical discussions of that period.[10] The Odessa consultation (1977) on "How does the Church teach authoritatively today?" addressed aspects of the hermeneutical problem, especially the question of continuity and change in the doctrinal tradition of the Church. Also, after Accra (1974), Faith and Order began to collect newer expressions of faith and hope from around the world. These were published in a series, and also summarized at Bangalore (1978) in "A Common Account of Hope". This work, which found continuation in the Faith and Order study on the Apostolic Faith, produced an awareness of the contextual aspects of confessions of faith, both in the sense of the original contexts in which they were made and of the effect on their use produced by the changing contexts of Christian discipleship.

20. The helpful results of these study processes did not prevent continuing conflicts, whether these were between traditions themselves, between the inherited traditions and newer contexts, or between various contextual approaches within each church or within the relationships of churches to one another. This was why Santiago felt the need to return once again to hermeneutical issues (cf. para. 11 above).

2. "According to the Scriptures"

21. The primary authority of Scripture within hermeneutical work is not weakened by our understanding of the way in which the text has been handed down within the Church through the process of transmission. The texts of Scripture thus received offer their revelatory character after a handing on through oral transmission. The written texts subsequently have been interpreted by means of diverse exegetical and scholarly methods. Wrestling with the principles and practice of interpretation, Faith and Order affirmed (Bristol, 1967/68) that the tools of modern exegetical scholarship are important if the biblical message is to speak with power and meaning today. These tools have contributed in vital ways to the present ecumenical convergence and growth in *koinonia*. The

---

[10] "The Authority of the Bible, Louvain, 1971" in: *The Bible. Its Authority and Interpretation in the Ecumenical Movement*, ed. Ellen Flesseman-van Leer, Faith and Order Paper No. 99, WCC Geneva 1983 (2nd edition), pp. 42-57.

exegetical exploration of the process of tradition within the Bible itself, together with the recognition of multiple interpretations of God's saving actions in history within the unity of the early apostolic church, points to ways the Word of God is expressed in human language and by human witness. This is to say, the Word of God is expressed in language and by witnesses shaped amid diverse situations of human life, which are historically, culturally and socially conceived. This is also to say: "The very nature of biblical texts means that interpreting them will require continued use of the historical-critical method,...[since] the Bible does not present itself as a direct revelation of timeless truths, but as the written testimony to a series of interventions in which God reveals himself in human history."[11] Though some churches and individual Christians reject historical-critical interpretation, common study of the Scriptures of the Old and New Testaments now has a long history of achieved agreement. Ecumenical hermeneutics can use the historical-critical method to establish, e.g., the background of the texts, the intentions of the authors, the inter-relationship of the different books.

22. Interpretation should not, however, depend only on this method, now shared by those of different traditions and theologies. Many other approaches to the text, both of long standing and of modern development, help in the recognition of the meaning of Scripture for the churches today and for the many different situations of the world Church. In particular the historical-critical method needs to be combined with a reading in critical interaction with experience, the experience both of individuals and of communities. Other methods are those inherent in traditional biblical interpretation including patristic, liturgical, homiletic, dogmatic and allegorical approaches to the text. Contemporary methods include those that focus on the original social setting of the texts (e.g. sociological methods); those that focus on the literary form of texts and the internal relationships within a text and between texts (e.g. semiotic and canonical methods); and those that focus on the potential of the text for readings generated by the encounter of the text with human reality (e.g. reader-response method). All these methods can also be used to deal

---

[11] The Interpretation of the Bible in the Church, Pontifical Biblical Commission 1993, p.128-129.

18

with extra-biblical sources. Some methods help to open up neglected dimensions of the past from the perspective of marginalized groups. Examples of the latter are feminist or liberationist analyses of systems of power and patronage.

23.   Nevertheless ecumenical hermeneutics cannot be reduced to the use of exegetical tools and methods isolated from the fullness of the experience of the interpreting community. A variety of factors are woven into that fullness, and these compose the hermeneutical locus within which Scripture is interpreted. These factors include oral tradition, narratives, memories and liturgies, as well as the life, teachings, and ethical decisions of the believing community. Thus, many dimensions of the life of the community are part of the context for interpreting the scriptural texts. Scripture emerges from episodes of life, a calendar of feasts, a scheme of history, and the witnessing account of the living people of God. In addition, Scripture becomes alive once again as it engages the life, feasts, history, and witness of faith communities today. From this perspective, the praxis of the Christian communities and people in different particular cultural and social contexts is itself a reading and an interpretation of the scriptural texts and not simply a position from which to approach the texts.

24.   Because the biblical texts originated in concrete historical situations, they witness to the salvific presence of the Triune God in those particular circumstances. However, the texts also transcend this particularity and become part of the world of the readers in each generation, of the witnessing community through the ages into the present. Although embedded in the life and times in which it was given written form, Scripture, as inspired testimony, provides a measure for the truth and meaning of human stories today. In this sense, hermeneutical priority belongs to the Word of God, which has critical authority over all traditions.

25.   The relation and sometimes also tension between past and present which exists when biblical texts are applied to our stories today reflects the eschatological dimension of Scripture itself. Just as Scripture constantly looks forward in hope to God's future, the interpreting activity

of the Church is also an anticipatory projection of the reality of the reign of God, which is both already present and yet to come. Reading "the signs of the times," both in the history of the past and in the events of the present, is to be done in the context of the announcement of "the new things to come"; this orientation to the future is part of the reality of the Church as an hermeneutical community.[12] Therefore the struggle for peace, justice, and the integrity of creation, the renewed sense of mission in witness and service, the liturgy in which the Church proclaims and celebrates the promise of God's reign and its coming in the praxis of the faith, are all integral parts of the constant interpretative task of the Church.

26. Ecumenical hermeneutics welcomes the diversity of insights that arise from biblical reflection of this broadly-based kind. A scriptural text may be considered as authoritative for a particular matter of faith or practice, even if this text is interpreted differently by the dialogue partners. Thus agreement may be reached concerning a responsibility laid upon the church even though different hermeneutical methods were employed in deriving this sense of responsibility from Scripture. On the other hand, the applicability of a text is not to be ruled out even if a specific interpretation is deemed by one of the dialogue partners to be irrelevant to a particular matter of faith or practice.

27. Common study of Scripture has achieved ecumenical advance. However, it has not by itself led to the visible unity of the Church. Interpreters from different churches and traditions have not been able to reach sufficient agreement for that. All Christians agree that Scripture holds a unique place in the shaping of Christian faith and practice. Most agree that the expression of apostolic faith is not confined to the formulation of that faith expressed in Scripture but that norms of faith have also been expressed in the life of the churches throughout the ages. The Church receives the texts of Scripture as part of the *paradosis* of the Gospel. The texts are to be respected as coming from outside to the interpreter to be engaged dialogically. In the process of interpretation, which involves the particular experiences of the reader, Scripture is the

---

[12] cf. below, Part C.

primary norm and criterion. Particular traditions need to be referred continuously to this norm by which they find their authenticity and validity. This response to Scripture takes shape communally and ecclesially in worship, in the sacramental life where hearing, touch and sight come together, in the *anamnesis* of the lives of biblical witnesses and in the lives of those who live the biblical message, inspired by the Holy Spirit. Scripture itself refers to the one Tradition, lived under the guidance of the Holy Spirit. The one Tradition, therefore, is the setting for the interpretation of Scripture.

3.   Interpreting the interpreters

28.   Within the one Tradition, as Christians engage with Scripture and their own traditions to understand God's will for the world and for the people called to be witnesses of God's love, they always need to interpret text and traditions anew. Amid this hermeneutical task, Christians are to be conscious that interpretations come out of special historical circumstances and that new issues may come out of various contexts. In considering these circumstances and issues, Christians involved in the hermeneutical task do well to investigate:

- the location from which the text is being interpreted;

- the choice of a specific text for interpretation;

- the involvement of power structures in the interpretation process;

- prejudices and presuppositions brought to bear on the interpretation process.

It is in the light of this understanding[13] that ecumenical hermeneutics needs to operate as a hermeneutics of coherence, showing the positive complementarity of traditions. It needs also to include a hermeneutics of suspicion. This does not mean the adoption of an attitude of mistrust but the application to oneself and one's dialogue partners of an approach which perceives how self-interest, power, national or ethnic or class or

---

[13]   cf. para. 6 above.

gender perspectives can affect the reading of texts and the understanding of symbols and practices. Positively, the recent work done by Protestants and Roman Catholics together on the Reformation debates about justification and sanctification has enabled fuller mutual understanding. Negatively, the way in which the Bible was used to justify apartheid is an example of a selective reading which was challenged by being confronted by these and other hermeneutical challenges. Safeguards against selective and prejudicial readings are also imperative in the realm of academic and scholarly interpretation, with particular attention to the wider testimony of Scripture and the experience of the many oppressed.

29.   Within the struggle for peace, justice, and the integrity of creation the hermeneutical dimension of the quest for reconciliation and unity can be painful, especially when reconciliation involves those whose common past has been marked by injustice or violence. Interpreting a history of this kind requires an hermeneutical awareness which enables one to renounce the stereotypes such histories can generate on both sides of a dispute. This hermeneutical process may call for repentance and forgiveness, since the reconciliation of injustice and violence requires a healing of memories, which is not the same as forgetfulness of the past. Much further work is clearly needed in this area of assessing the past. One must pray for the miracle of resurrection to new life, even if the marks of the crucifixion remain.

30.   Hermeneutics in the service of unity must also proceed on the presumption that those who interpret the Christian tradition differently each have "right intention of faith".[14] It is not only a condition of dialogue, but a fruitful product of dialogue, that the partners come to appreciate and trust one another`s sincerity and good intention. This means each is sincerely seeking to transmit that which God wishes to pass on through the Church. It is important in conveying results of dialogue to the churches to transmit also the sense of mutual confidence. This is especially so where a painful shared history of conflict calls for the healing of memories. Since diversity can be an expression of the rich gifts of the Holy Spirit, the churches are called to become aware of the possibility of

---

[14] cf. BEM, Ministry 52.

an abiding complementarity, i.e., of the values inherent in the "otherness" of one another and even of the right to be different from each other, when such differences are part of the exploration of the divine mystery and the divinely-willed unity. Viewed in this way, differences can be an invitation and a starting point for the common search for the truth, in a spirit of *koinonia* that entails a disposition to *metanoia*, under the guidance of the Spirit of God.

31. When differences of interpretation and possible complementarity are being assessed, the question of authoritative interpretation arises. Part of the ecumenical method is to ensure that the partners in dialogue are made aware where authority resides in each church and how it is being understood and received by each participant. The process of ecumenical hermeneutics involves not only faithful understanding and interpretation of texts, symbols and practices but also analysis of the relative weight given to those texts, symbols and practices by the various churches in respect of the authoritative nature of sources themselves and the interpretations derived from them. Clarity about authority is a crucial element in that dimension of hermeneutics which concentrates on the faithful communication and reception of the meaning of texts, symbols and practices. Consequently, the relationship between Scripture, Tradition and traditions and Christian experience arising from liturgical and other practices needs to be dealt with again and again within the hermeneutical process.

4. One Tradition and many traditions

32. The "one Tradition" signifies the redeeming presence of the resurrected Christ from generation to generation abiding in the community of faith, while the "many traditions" are particular modes and manifestations of that presence. God's self-disclosure transcends all expressions of it. How can Christians and churches share in the gift of the one Tradition as they confess and live according to Scripture? How are they to read their own traditions in the light of the one Tradition? As has been noted above, the Fourth World Conference addressed the issue of hermeneutics in an ecumenical perspective, opening up the many

traditions to the recognition of the one Tradition as a gift from God. Recognition of and continuity with the one Tradition, however, should not be confused with a mere repetition of the past without any recognition of the present. The Holy Spirit inspires and leads the churches each to rethink and reinterpret their tradition in conversation with each other, always aiming to embody the one Tradition in the unity of God's Church. The churches of God as living communities, constituted by faith in Jesus Christ and empowered by the Holy Spirit, must always re-receive the Gospel in ways that relate to their present experience of life. It is in this process of re-reception that the minds of Christian communities are enlightened by the Holy Spirit to discern truth from falsehood and to acknowledge both the richness and the limitedness of the diverse geographical, historical, religious and social circumstances in which the Gospel is made manifest. Ecumenical hermeneutics is not an unaided human enterprise. It is an ecclesial act led by the Spirit and therefore it should be carried out in a setting of prayer.

33. The churches involved in the ecumenical movement recognize that by being in conversation with each other they learn to appreciate mutually each other's gifts, as well as to challenge limited or false understandings of what God expects churches to be and to do in the world. Thus they begin to move from identifying themselves in opposition to one another to identifying themselves in relation to one another. This opening to new understandings of the traditions of other churches - their history, their liturgies, their martyrs and saints, their sacraments and ministries - has changed the ecumenical climate since Montreal. The exchange of biblical exegesis, of systematic theological approaches, of historiographical studies, and practical-theological projects, has been a very enriching development. Exegetical research is undertaken on the basis of receptive as well as critical interconfessional discussion, fostered by ecumenical dialogue. Bible translations and commentaries have been published ecumenically, common liturgical calendars, lectionaries, hymn and prayer books have become the means of sharing spiritual resources with one another.

34. This ecumenical sharing has indeed created a new ecumenical situation, characterized by growth in mutual understanding across

confessional boundaries predicated on a new appreciation of particular confessional traditions and witness. The challenge to move on from mutual understanding to mutual recognition is now before the churches in the search for visible unity. For example, ecumenical hermeneutics must also enable dialogue partners to declare their particular understanding of the relationship between "continuity" and "discontinuity" in the historic expression of the faith of the people of God. As one instance, the Reformation introduced changes in ministerial order which the Reformers perceived as a return to continuity with the early church whereas others felt the changes were an example of discontinuity.

35. Traditions are transmitted orally as well as through written texts. Ecumenical hermeneutics - as every hermeneutical task - is therefore a dynamic process concerned not only with written sources but also with oral tradition. In addition to textual and oral tradition, meaning is conveyed through non-verbal symbols: Christian art and music, liturgical gestures or colours, icons, the creation and use of sacred space and time, Christian symbols or signs are important aspects of the way in which the various dialogue partners understand and communicate their faith. Ecumenical hermeneutics needs to be intentional about incorporating this rich, but also neglected, source material for interpretation, communication and reception. As with symbols, Christian practices need to be taken into consideration by those engaged in ecumenical hermeneutics. Even when there is a basis for theological convergence on the meaning of, e.g. baptism or eucharist, attention needs to be given to the practices surrounding these rites in particular ecclesial communities. Here as elsewhere, hermeneutical reflection can serve as an aid in the process of recognizing the same faith underlying different practices.

36. As well as recognizing the new ecumenical situation, churches are also becoming more and more aware of shifts in perception and reception among their members which arise from changes in the media of communication. Spoken words and visual images are especially significant in the increasingly powerful multimedia culture of today's world. A renewed appreciation of narrative forms of transmission sheds new light on processes of interpretation and communication. It is also

important to draw critically upon the perceptions of secular artists and film producers as they take up themes and symbols from Christian history.

37. Yet ultimately, amid the many ecclesial traditions, the one Tradition is revealed in the living presence of Christ in the world, but is not something to be captured and controlled by human discourse. It is a living, eschatological reality, eluding all attempts at a final linguistic definition and conceptual disclosure. One way of describing the one Tradition is by speaking about the ecclesial capacity of *receiving* revelation. This capacity is nothing less than the gift of the Holy Spirit, received by the apostles at Pentecost and given to every Christian community and to every member of the community in the process of Christian initiation. This capacity is the gift of the Holy Spirit who "will guide you into all the truth" (Jn 16:13), who is the Spirit of truth; that truth is Jesus Christ himself (Jn 14:6), the perfect image of the Father from whom the Spirit proceeds. The capacity to receive the fullness of revelation is actualized in the Church's celebration of the eucharist, which involves both a hearing and an embodying of the Word of God, a participation in the *eschaton*, the feast of the kingdom.

B. ONE GOSPEL IN MANY CONTEXTS

1.   Living in diverse contexts

38.   Christian communities live in particular places and times, defined culturally, economically, politically and religiously. These are the contexts in which their faith is lived and the Gospel is interpreted and proclaimed. The diversity of contexts in which the churches live calls for engagement with the diverse riches of Scripture. In other words, diverse contexts inform the selection, as well as the specific interpretation, of Scripture. Selected passages of Scripture, in turn, may challenge as well as affirm diverse contexts:

*   In a context of social injustice, Mary's Magnificat (Lk 1:46-55; cf. 1 Sam 2:1-10) and Jesus' inaugural sermon (Lk 4:18, quoting Is 42:7) may become a word of hope for the poor and the oppressed. And, at the same time, these may be a word of judgement to oppressors.

*   In a context where Christians are a tiny minority among people of other faiths, the affirmation of the common humanity of all women and men as created in God's image may turn attention to the presence of the Spirit outside the Christian churches. As reflected in the story of Paul's sermon in Athens (Acts 17:16ff.), this awareness of common humanity and of the Spirit's presence may be both affirming and challenging in relation to peoples of other living faith traditions.

*   In a context of resurgent nationalism, Jesus' commandment to love even our enemies (Mt 5:44; cf. Lev.19:34) and to distinguish between loyalty to God and the emperor (Mk 12:17) may at once challenge the inherent danger of nations becoming exclusive and totalitarian, and affirm the Christian responsibility to upbuild or rebuild the nations by and for the sake of the participation and reconciliation of all people (Rom 13:5-10).

*   In a context of what some call postmodern pluralism, where individual choice is so emphasized that common points of reference are obscured, an affirmation of commitment and of communion

may become life-giving. This affirmation need not deny the value of personal freedom but rather recognizes the tension Paul addresses when he wrote to the Corinthians: "'All things are lawful', but not all things build up. Do not seek your own advantage, but that of the other" (1Cor 10:23f.).

39. Dialogue among Christian communities of different confessions as well as contexts calls for respect and openness. Partners are, first of all, called to respect one another, recognizing the temptation to reduce one another to one's own confessional categories or to the cultural, economic, political, and religious categories that interweave to define one's own context. This call entails an openness to *metanoia*. Such openness includes a willingness to see the limitations of one's own perspective as well as to listen actively to and communicate with one's own dialogue partners. Encounters characterized by respect and openness are often enriching. These encounters may also give rise to disagreements that become conflictual.

40. Amid these complex interactions, Christian churches should welcome faithful and fruitful encounters of the Gospel and contexts. Churches should also recognize and repent of false interpretations of the Gospel that may be occasioned by contextual influences. This is to say that while the Gospel proclaimed in local languages and music and customs may enliven people's faith, there are also contexts in which racist ideologies and their attendant political institutions have been justified by churches and said to be compatible with the Gospel. Likewise, churches and societies have both, consciously and unconsciously, discriminated against or oppressed women in contradiction to the Gospel's message of liberation for all people. Wherever the Gospel is authentically engaged by diverse cultures, its interpretation and proclamation will be life-giving for men and women, young and old, sick and healthy, rich and poor, uneducated and educated.

41. Missionary activity especially exemplifies the complex interactions of churches and contexts. Some Christian missionaries have greatly helped local peoples and societies to affirm and express themselves in their own cultural media. Others have been reluctant or unable to engage local contexts and peoples respectfully and openly. Historically, many

missionaries were bound up with imperialist impulses and consequently became colonialist. Christianity has continued to be alien and alienating in many places, even as it has initiated life-giving change in many other places. In every context there is a potential ambiguity about the way in which the gospel is proclaimed. Every Christian community needs to repent of what is alienating in the way in which the gospel continues to be proclaimed and to re-commit themselves to ensuring that the gospel that is proclaimed is life-giving.

42.   All these encounters make it clear just how complex are the interactions within and among diverse confessions and contexts. Contextual differences have helped shape confessional divisions. Correlatively, communities of the same confessional family have taken on different faces in different contexts. For example, it makes a great difference whether a church has long been present in a country where it is a majority or whether it is made up of migrants living in another country. Moreover, confessionally different communities have reacted differently to the same context in which they are living together. Some have opposed particular forms of nationalism; others have legitimized and supported them. Although these examples turn attention to contextual challenges, confessional challenges do not disappear. Indeed, it is important to recognize the ways in which new churches have arisen precisely because of different responses to particular contextual challenges.

2.   Contextuality and catholicity

43.   The many local communities of Christians throughout the world, each within their own context, perceive themselves as embodiments of the one catholic Church. They belong to one another in a profound way because of their relationship to God through Jesus Christ. They make up one family, having been "born of water and the Spirit" (Jn 3:5). For the Apostle Paul, this unity is rooted in Jesus himself. He therefore challenges the Corinthians to avoid factions by asking them: "Is Christ divided?" (1Cor 1:13). Later, in the same letter, Paul compares the Christian communities to the members of a body, each one needing the others, none enjoying special status above the rest (cf. 1Cor 12:12-26).

This unity and diversity of Christian communities flows together from the Holy Spirit. It is one and the same Spirit who bestows the marvelous variety of gifts and ministries (cf. 1Cor 12:1-11). These gifts and ministries work together to build up the bonds of faith and love which allow the Church to grow in communion day by day, until the full realization of communion in the kingdom of God.

44.   In order to reflect theologically upon both the diversity of and the relationships among local Christian communities, the terms "contextuality" and "catholicity" are especially helpful. The dimension of *contextuality* refers to the interpretation and the proclamation of the gospel within the life and culture of a specific people and community. Such a proclamation of the gospel can seek to judge the cultural context, it can seek to separate itself from the culture in which the church is set and it can seek to transform culture. As the WCC Jerusalem Consultation "On Intercultural Hermeneutics" stated, contextuality "appears whenever the gospel works like salt and leaven, not overwhelming a context, but permeating and enlivening it in distinctive ways. When the church's faith is genuinely contextual, the shame and stigma imposed on oppressed people begins to be lifted. They find a new dignity as they see not only their own lives but also their culture in God's redeeming light. When faith is contextual, there is a recognition that the gospel speaks to Christians in their language, connects with their symbols, addresses their needs and awakens their creative energies."[15]

45.   The term *catholicity* derives from the Greek words *kath' holon*, which mean "according to the whole". This word refers to the fullness, integrity and totality of life in Christ and the inclusiveness and wholeness of the Christian community.[16] Catholicity, according to the ancient creeds, is one of the primary qualities of the Church. It is ascribed, first of all, to each local community, inasmuch as each community expresses in its faith,

---

[15] *International Review of Mission* 85 (1996) No. 337, p. 245.

[16]   These senses of "catholicity" have been accounted for in the modern ecumenical movement; cf. e.g., "The Holy Spirit and the Catholicity of the Church" in Norman Goodall (ed.), *The Uppsala Report 1968: Official Report of the Fourth Assembly of the World Council of Churches, Uppsala July 4-20, 1968*, WCC Geneva 1968.

life, and witness this fullness that is not yet fully realized. Churches are called to grow in God's gift of catholicity by engaging one another in collegial and conciliar structures, by mutual accountability to the Gospel, and by prayer for the eschatological work of the Holy Spirit. As churches look forward to the future of eschatological promise, they also look back to the apostolic community assembled on the morning of Pentecost. This sense of catholicity across the ages, as well as among local Christian communities of diverse contexts in any given age, sustains hope for the full realization of common life in Christ.

46. By its very nature, the eucharist is to be the celebration of a local community and the manifestation of its unity; at the same time it expresses the communion of the local church with other churches that celebrate the same eucharist and with all those who have celebrated it throughout the ages. Thus the local church experiences the fulness of the Church, the catholicity of the Church. Therefore, the eucharistic celebration itself urges every church, on the one hand, to share the needs and hopes of the people in the place where it lives and to speak their language, and, on the other hand, to overcome the divisions that prevent the common celebration of the Lord's supper, in order to enjoy the unity for which Jesus prayed (Jn 17:21).

47. To speak of contextuality and catholicity together clarifies the relationship between the local community and the wider communion of all local communities. Contextual interpretations can contribute to a fuller interpretation of the Gospel and can thereby speak to the Christian community as a whole. When an interpretation of the Gospel in a particular context points to injustice or to liberation, this interpretation is not simply a contextual claim. It may provide an insight to be tested and amended or applied in other contexts. Accordingly, catholicity binds all local communities together, thereby allowing them to contribute to one another's understandings and to broaden their horizons.

48. Interpretation of the Gospel has to be relevant to particular believing communities in particular contexts in order to be both pastoral and prophetic. But no interpretation can claim to be absolute. All must be aware of the limitations of any perspective or position. The catholicity

31

that binds communities together makes possible this awareness of limitation as well as a mutual acknowledgment of contribution to one another's interpretation. In this way, catholicity enables communities to free one another from one-sidedness or from over-emphasis on only one aspect of the Gospel. Catholicity enables communities to liberate one another from being blinded or bound by any one context and so to embody across and among diverse contexts the solidarity that is a special mark of Christian *koinonia*.

C. THE CHURCH AS AN HERMENEUTICAL COMMUNITY

1. Ecclesial discernment and the truth of the Gospel

49. This ongoing dialogue involving both catholicity and contextuality characterizes the Church as a "hermeneutical community". The Church, whether embodied in a local congregation, episcopal diocese, or a Christian World Communion, is called to interpret texts, symbols and practices so as to discern the Word of God as a word of life amid ever-changing times and places. This hermeneutical task undertaken by the Church, with the guidance of the Holy Spirit, is a condition for apostolic mission in and for the world. To speak of the Church as an hermeneutical community is also to say that this community is a proper locus for the interpretation and the proclamation of the Gospel.

50. Hermeneutics, perhaps especially ecumenical hermeneutics, is not the work of specialists. Ecumenical hermeneutics, in the pursuit of visible church unity, is first and foremost the work of the whole people gathered in believing communities in diverse contexts. Believers, pastors, theologians, and biblical exegetes, each have distinctive gifts to bring to the hermeneutical task. These gifts are most appropriately brought together and exercised within the various settings in which the Church carries out its work as an hermeneutical community.

51. For the sake of this work, churches need to renew their responsibility for the formation of their members as faithful hearers and interpreters. This formation is embedded in the life of worship[17] and is nurtured by conciliar teaching, the writings of the early church, and the witness of saints and martyrs. All these testimonies to the apostolic faith disclose the faithful and fruitful interpretation of God's word through Christian history. They also testify to the ways in which non-theological issues, e.g., the struggle to attain or maintain ecclesiastical or political power, may influence or distort interpretation. Finally, these witnesses teach that temporary divisions may in the end, in God's time, be more

---

[17] cf. *So We Believe, So We Pray: Towards Koinonia in Worship*, Thomas F. Best and Dagmar Heller (eds.), WCC Geneva, 1995.

interesting

fruitful for mutual and respectful understanding than an enforcement of unity when and where there is no unity. Such a formation will enable believers of diverse confessions and contexts to enter into respectful and open relationships. With the Spirit's guidance, these relationships may lead to fruitful dialogue concerning the interpretation of the Gospel, as well as concerning the interpretation of ecumenical documents dedicated to the search for visible church unity.

52. The Church as hermeneutical community must beware of false interpretations of the Gospel that may have life-denying contextual consequences, for example, interpretations legitimizing racism or economic exploitation as noted above. The Church as hermeneutical community must also beware of false interpretations of the Gospel that threaten or destroy the fullness of life together in Christ. At the same time, faithful interpretation of the Gospel also may give rise to conflict and critical tension, both within believing communities and between the Church and the world. The Church is called to offer a pastoral response to those who doubt or who raise disturbing questions and to those who suffer amid deep disagreements. The Church thereby carries out the ministry of reconciliation to which it is called.

53. Ecumenical hermeneutics takes as its starting point the reality that conversations aiming at greater unity are carried out by representatives of the various churches and that their contributions are mediated through particular ecclesial, cultural, social, economic, geographical and historical backgrounds.

- For dialogue to be genuine, these representatives need to see each other as equal partners.

- They must, on the one hand, speak to each other from the perspective of their traditional interpretations of the apostolic faith as articulated in their confessional documents, their liturgies and their experience.

- But they must do so with a willingness to view their own interpretations from the vantage point of those with whom they are in dialogue. This involves being attentive to the insights provided by the dialogue partner, taking care to take into account one's own unwitting prejudices and limited perspectives.

2. Authority, apostolicity and mutual accountability

54. The Church as an hermeneutical community is responsible for the faithful transmission of the inherited Gospel in different times and places. In that process the Holy Spirit guides the churches in discerning, receiving and communicating the will of God in the ever-changing circumstances of life. The churches have developed in their histories specific and differentiated ministerial structures by which they preserve their apostolicity, unity and mission. Despite the different configurations of these ministerial structures that the churches have developed in their separation from each other, it is widely recognized that ministerial structures must serve the purpose of the Church, to lead all into unity with God by the power of the Holy Spirit.

55. The Holy Spirit maintains the churches of God in truth and guides all the faithful into unity with Jesus Christ (Jn 16:13), distributes the ministry of Christ to all believers and empowers them to participate in God's mission for the salvation of the world. All ministries in the Church are related to each other and their authority is derived from their identification with Christ's ministry. In the ongoing ecclesiology discussion of Faith and Order it has been affirmed that the Church is a communion of co-responsible persons. No function, no gift, no charisma is exercised outside or above this communion. All are related through the one Spirit in the one Body. All believers, because of their unity with Jesus Christ and the indwelling of the Holy Spirit, have the potential to receive God's word, to discern God's will, and to proclaim the Gospel. Those whose call by God to exercise the ministry of oversight (*episkopé*) is recognized by the church must enable the people of God to recognize and actualize the gifts that the Holy Spirit has bestowed upon them for the fulfilment of the church's life and mission. This means that the ministry of oversight must include an hermeneutical function. The vitality of the church's life and mission depends upon the actualization of these gifts.

56. While the Holy Spirit distributes the ministry of Christ to all believers, the same Spirit unites all ministries by means of the ministry of *episkopé*. The function of *episkopé* is to sustain and nourish the unity of the local church, to maintain its communion in faith, life and witness with all other local churches; to safeguard the apostolicity and catholicity of the local church; and to empower the local church to discern God's will, to proclaim the Gospel and to be a credible witness of God's presence in the world. Although the forms of *episkopé* have developed differently within various ecclesial traditions, the functions of such a ministry have been widely recognized to be of fundamental importance for ecclesial unity. Christian churches continue to explore the appropriate forms of *episkopé* for this unity. As is the case with all ministries, *episkopé* can only be exercised within and in relation to the whole Church. It needs, as all other ministries, the recognition, collaboration, support and assent of the whole community. The authority of *episkopé* is grounded upon the authority of Christ's sacrificial love and humility (Lk 22:25-27). If *episkopé* becomes oppressive, overlooks the charisms or hinders rightful communication among the ministries, it becomes an exercise of power alien to the authority of Christ.

57. An important visible expression of the unity of God's Church occurs whenever those who have been entrusted with the oversight of the churches are gathered to support one another, to strengthen and give account of the faith, life and witness that unites them in Christ. Collegiality is at work wherever those entrusted with oversight gather, discern, speak and act as one on behalf of the whole church. This entails leading the church by means of the wisdom gained by corporate prayer, study and reflection, drawing on Scripture, tradition and reason with attention to the wisdom and experience of all church communities and of the contemporary world. Such collegial exercise of oversight is exercised at the present time by those churches who are united in faith, life and service to the world. In some parts of the world, the ecumenical movement has encouraged and brought into existence shared oversight on

matters of Christian faith and witness by churches who are not yet visibly united.[18]

58. The ecumenical recognition that those who have been baptized in the name of the Triune God are brought into unity with Christ, with each other and with the Church of every time and place challenges the churches to overcome their divisions and visibly manifest their communion in faith and in all aspects of Christian life and witness. Towards the realization of this goal, churches are encouraged to increase their consultation with other churches, at all levels, regarding important questions of faith and discipline. Any church which is not prepared to listen to the voices of other churches runs the danger of missing the truth of the Spirit as it operates in the other churches.

59. Within the ecumenical movement, a number of structures which foster encounters between divided churches help them work together as a common hermeneutical community characterized by mutual accountability. For example, the various areas of activity within the World Council of Churches provide a wide range of opportunities for common interpretation and praxis of the gospel message. Bilateral relationships concerned with theological dialogue, work for justice, peace and the integrity of creation and collaboration in mission, education and charitable works, offer similar opportunities. As churches find these and other means of communion across confessional and cultural lines fruitful, they may also benefit by improving communication with their own community.

60. An ecumenical exercise of teaching authority is already beginning to develop in some respects. It is hoped that ways of common decision making can be developed, even as there is allowance for certain decisions a church must take without or even against the opinion of others. All must be aware of the fact that new expressions of the faith often emerge from the talents and needs of a local church. Accordingly, the need for

---

[18] A useful report on emerging patterns of shared oversight can be found in the forthcoming Faith and Order report on *Episkopé and Episcopacy Within the Quest for Visible Unity*.

decisive judgments from time to time at local or regional levels must be acknowledged. It is, after all, the local churches which are challenged directly by the possibilities and the failures of their contexts and cultures. There is a need to hold together the freedom for diverse expressions and the necessity to confess together for the sake of unity, in the spirit of mutual love and patience.

61. The Christian churches cherish their conciliar tradition which goes back to their very beginning (Acts 15). They have come together in synods and councils throughout the centuries. The ecumenical movement considers its dialogues and preliminary structures of deliberation and consultation to be not only instruments for the fulfilment of its hermeneutical task but also a patient preparation for coming together in a genuine ecumenical council able to restore full *koinonia* as God wills. Ecumenical dialogues and deliberative consultations are, in this preliminary and preparatory sense, aspects of the Church's conciliarity. Ecumenical structures may already help churches communicate to one another decisions taken in matters of faith and discipline, and to prepare for decisions to be made, so that what relates to all should be dealt with by all. Such gradual steps prepare the churches for sharing common structures of decision making, as well as for engaging the significant qualities of their diverse modes of authoritative teaching.

62. The quality of the churches' authoritative teaching depends very much upon commonly accepted hermeneutical procedures with regard to the traditions and formulations inherited from the past. Mutual knowledge of the criteriological principles guiding one another's authoritative teaching (cf. footnote 8) is an important contribution to mutual understanding. It is to be hoped that these developments will, in God's time, help the churches together to make decisive judgments in matters of faith. After due reception, these judgements may become part of their common witness, according to Scripture. More work needs to be done to find common ground on which to test the authoritative nature of the teaching.

3. Reception as an hermeneutical process

63.   The search for the unity of Christians divided by cultural or social differences, or by the separate development of confessions and denominations, requires attentive reception of each other. This reception, in turn, requires recognition of the dignity of all as human beings and, within the Christian community, as sisters and brothers in Christ. This mutual reception by Christians amid cultural, social and confessional differences is addressed by Apostle Paul when he writes: "Therefore receive one another, as Christ also has received us to the glory of God" (Rom 15:7). The hermeneutical implications of this reception of one another are manifold and bear upon the way churches relate to one another's traditions of texts, symbols, rites and practices. Reception of ecumenical agreements thus involves the reception of other persons; it may require a transformation of one's own life and of relations with others.

64.   The Church is a communion of persons in relation; thus active participation and dialogue between communities, and within each community at all levels, is one expression of the Church's nature. The divine being of the Triune God is the source and the exemplar of communion. The Holy Spirit is sent to create communion bestowing the gift of faith upon each believer. Likewise, the Holy Spirit empowers each one to understand more fully the revealed Word of God and to apply it more fruitfully to the concrete situations of daily life. As a "royal priesthood" (1Pet 2:9), the community of the baptized engages in the active reception of the Gospel. Churches acknowledge the need to consult all levels of their constituency in matters of doctrine. Historically, even the reception of ecumenical councils was a process that extended through a considerable period of time, and employed a wide variety of means, such as the liturgy, catechesis, theology, the teaching of pastors, and popular piety. This process of reception called upon the participation of all church members, according to the charisms and ministries of each.

65.   In recent times, growing agreements between the churches have improved the climate for mutual consultation, reception and

accountability. At the same time, the reception of these agreements in some churches has been far from complete. The reception of ecumenical documents, which have the distinct purpose of helping to reunify divided Christian communities, is part of the ecumenical task of the Church as an hermeneutical community. The process of responses to BEM, for example, sheds light on this form of reception, indicating in particular the diversity of criteria by which churches read and evaluate ecumenical documents. The BEM responses further show that reception is more than simply a church's official response to a document. Churches were asked to respond not only to a text, but beyond that to consider changes in their own life and finally to change in their relations with others who could also recognize in the text the faith of the Church through the ages. Reception is therefore also a process that extends over time and involves many factors, including a certain level of ecumenical education, the accessibility of the texts, resources for their distribution and help of theologians and local ministers to explicate their content and implications. The forums on bilateral dialogues have contributed much to a more adequate understanding of these factors.[19]

66. A practical application of ecumenical hermeneutics occurs both in the production and reception of ecumenical documents. It is important to recognize, however, an important difference between these two spheres. Ecumenical documents are *written* jointly in the context of active discussion during which the dialogue partners may question each other with regard to respective interpretations, challenging each other's positions and developing insights that point to convergence. On the other hand, ecumenical documents are *read* by people who must enter into the dialogue without having been part of the initial discussion and who did not have the opportunity to present their own views in their own terms or to check their perceptions of the views being presented by others. Moreover, ecumenical documents are often produced through multilateral dialogue, whereas these documents are normally read from the point of view of a single tradition. Consequently, it is crucial that special care is taken by those who produce ecumenical documents to

---

[19] cf. esp. *Sixth Forum on Bilateral Dialogues,* Faith and Order Paper No. 168, 1995.

ensure that meaningful exchange is facilitated at all levels by adequate attention to those dimensions of ecumenical hermeneutics that result in accurate communication and reception.

CONCLUSION

67. Under the power of the Holy Spirit the Church is intended to be God's special instrument for bringing about the encounter between the Word of Life and human beings. When this Word is received, it nourishes as the living bread, which "gives life to the world," for which Jesus' listeners asked: "Lord, give us this bread always" (Jn 6:33-34).

68. In and through diverse historical and contemporary forms of inculturation and contextualization the bread of life, which is to be broken and distributed, remains one bread. Although the Word enters history, this historicity does not limit it to any single historical form or formulation. Yet this insight leads neither to limitless diversity nor to ecumenical complacency. Rather, as an hermeneutical community, the Church is called to grow into full *koinonia* by Spirit-guided discernment of the living Tradition. The Church should not be imprisoned by holding on to inadequate answers from the past, nor should it silence the Word of God by endlessly putting off a clear recognition of the way this Word continues to impart meaning and orientation for human life. Under the guidance of the Holy Spirit, in faithfulness to the living Tradition, and through genuine ecumenical forms of conciliar deliberation and reception, the Church is called to "interpret the signs of the times" (Mt 16:3) by looking to the One who is both in and beyond time, to the One "who is the same, yesterday, today and forever" (Heb 13:8).